Spirit of Christmas

A Children's Musical

A light-hearted look at the true meaning of Christmas

Kate Doherty

We hope you enjoy *Spirit of Christmas*.
Further copies are available from your local music shop or
Christian bookshop.

In case of difficulty, please contact the publisher direct:

The Sales Department
KEVIN MAYHEW LTD
Buxhall
Stowmarket
Suffolk IP14 3BW

Phone 01449 737978
Fax 01449 737834
E-mail info@kevinmayhewltd.com

Public performance of this work is allowed only with the permission of the publisher and on condition that the appropriate performance royalty is paid. Enquiries should be made to the Copyright department, Kevin Mayhew Ltd.

First published in Great Britain in 1999 by Kevin Mayhew Ltd.

© Copyright 1999 Kevin Mayhew Ltd.

ISBN 1 84003 390 8
ISMN M 57004 571 6
Catalogue No: 1450140

0 1 2 3 4 5 6 7 8 9

The text and music in this book are protected by copyright and may not be reproduced in any way for sale or private use without the consent of the copyright owner.

Cover design by Jonathan Stroulger

Music arranged by Keith Stent

Music setting: Geoffrey Moore
Editing and typesetting: Margaret Lambeth

Spirit of Christmas
A children's musical
by Kate Doherty

Characters

Narrator

Noel — the mysterious Christmas visitor

Matthew — a little boy who befriends Noel

Old Grumpy — a shabby old man living in Matthew's street

Mitzi — a spoilt, over-indulged little girl; neighbour of Matthew

Mrs Never-In — Mitzi's mother; a tireless shopper, shops 'until she drops'

Mrs High and Mighty — a neighbour who is rather snobbish

Mrs Next-Door — another neighbour; a catering victim who plans to have 'twenty-one for dinner'

Eileen — Matthew's mother

Jan — Matthew's father

Children — Matthew's friends

Setting the scene

The script reflects the fact that this play was first performed in a church. Scenery, therefore, had to be static and there were no scene changes during the play. Five gable outlines represented a street of houses, each one appropriately 'furnished' with a few items. A travelling spotlight lit each house as its occupant(s) came into focus in the script. It is useful for the direction of the play to have the stage set at two levels. In the first performance the stage was divided by several shallow steps, with the houses on a higher level.

Scene 1

Narrator Our story takes place in a street not far from here, but not quite over there. It happens at a time when past and future meet. And it all begins the day before Christmas Eve. A boy called Matthew is on his way home from a Christmas party . . .

(Stage in darkness. Robust chorus of 'We wish you a Merry Christmas' which dies out as centre stage is lit and Matthew walks into the light. His paper hat is askew and he's trailing a balloon behind him.)

Matthew I'll *have* to have a rest. I'm *worn out* with Christmas parties. *(Sighs)* I've been to *four* this week! *(Sinks down on steps)*

(Enter Noel with clipboard, pen poised. He walks past Matthew, staring at houses, makes notes, walks back – looks down at Matthew)

Noel Hello. You don't look very happy. What's wrong?

Matthew *(Startled)* Where did you come from?

Noel Never mind that. Now tell me what's wrong?

Matthew I'm tired. *(Balloon escapes)* Too many parties – and it's not even Christmas yet.

Noel *(Sits down beside Matthew. Recovers balloon and gives it back)* I'm a bit tired too. I've been tramping round the streets all day, knocking on doors . . .

Matthew *(Interested)* Are you selling things, or getting people to try soap powder or something?

Noel *(Laughing)* No, No! *(He holds out the clipboard)* I'm doing a sort of – erm, *survey* on Christmas. You know, what Christmas means to people.

Matthew *(Hugging his knees and becoming interested)* Then what? I mean, when you've finished?

Noel *(Getting up)* Questions, questions! I think we should introduce ourselves. *(Extends hand)* I'm Noel. Pleased to meet you.

Matthew *(Shakes Noel's hand)* And I'm Matthew and I can help you with your survey – I know *everybody* in this street *(waves arms expansively)*.

Noel *(Smiling)* All right. You can show me around. It'll save time, and maybe you can help me to find the Spirit of Christmas – because that's really what I'm looking for.

Matthew What's that? – the Spirit of Christmas?

Noel Aha! When I find it your question will be answered.

(Children gather at one side of stage)

Matthew *(dragging Noel by the hand)* C'mon. All my pals are back from the party. They know all about Christmas – 'cos they're *children*. Start with them.

Narrator And so, Noel spoke to the children. Instead of answering his questions, they told him they'd sing a song about Christmas.

THAT'S CHRISTMAS

1. Robins in the holly tree,
   sleigh bells in the snow,
   hot mince-pies and Christmas pud,
   people dashing to and fro.
   Santa in the chimney,
   toys galore below.
   All the things that we enjoy;
   Hooray – that's Christmas!

2. Holly wreaths upon the door,
   lights upon the tree,
   parties, games and dancing,
   fun for you and me,
   gifts in pretty parcels,
   reindeer prancing by;
   all the things that we enjoy,
   Hooray – that's Christmas!

(Song taken twice through. Second time, a few children skip and dance across front of stage (including Matthew) in time to music. As they do, Old Grumpy bursts out of his house and struggles down the steps in front of the children)

That's Christmas

1. Ro-bins in the hol-ly tree, sleigh bells in the snow, peo-ple dash-ing to and fro. San-ta in the chim-ney, toys ga-lore be-low; all the things that we en-joy: Hoo-ray – that's Christ-mas!

2. Hol-ly wreaths up-on the door, lights up-on the tree, fun for you and me, gifts in pret-ty par-cels, rein-deer pranc-ing by;

© Copyright 1999 Kevin Mayhew Ltd.
It is illegal to photocopy music.

Old Grumpy *(bellows)* Be quiet! Stop that noise! Get away from my door – *now*!

(Children stop singing, draw back. Noel comes over)

Noel They didn't mean to upset you. They're only children – and it's Christmas.

Old Grumpy *(Turns on Noel)* Christmas? I *hate* Christmas. *(Children gradually withdraw, leaving Matthew with Noel)* Only children? They're *pests*. *Noisy pests*!

(He turns to go up the steps, stumbles, drops his stick. Matthew recovers it, tries to help him)

Old Grumpy *(Snatching stick)* Mind your own business! I don't need your help.

(Noel takes Matthew's hand, and they make their way back towards the children. They're discussing the incident)

Child 1 That's Old Grumpy – he's *horrible*! *(A murmur of agreement)*

Child 2 He hates us all. Well, we'll just be horrible right back. We'll throw snowballs at his window and –

Noel No. He's just sad because nobody's shown him love for a long, long time. Love's a wonderful thing. But it's a strange thing too – if no one shows you love, after a while you can't accept even the tiniest bit when it's offered to you – like a man who's starving. Offer him food and he can scarcely eat.

Child 1 Love? That's all soppy, isn't it?

(Children laugh – Noel sits down beside them)

Noel No, no. I mean loving your neighbour – loving others in the way Jesus wants us to do. Remember – love is in the little things. Let me tell you about it –

LOVE IS IN THE LITTLE THINGS

LOVE IS IN THE LITTLE THINGS *continued ...*

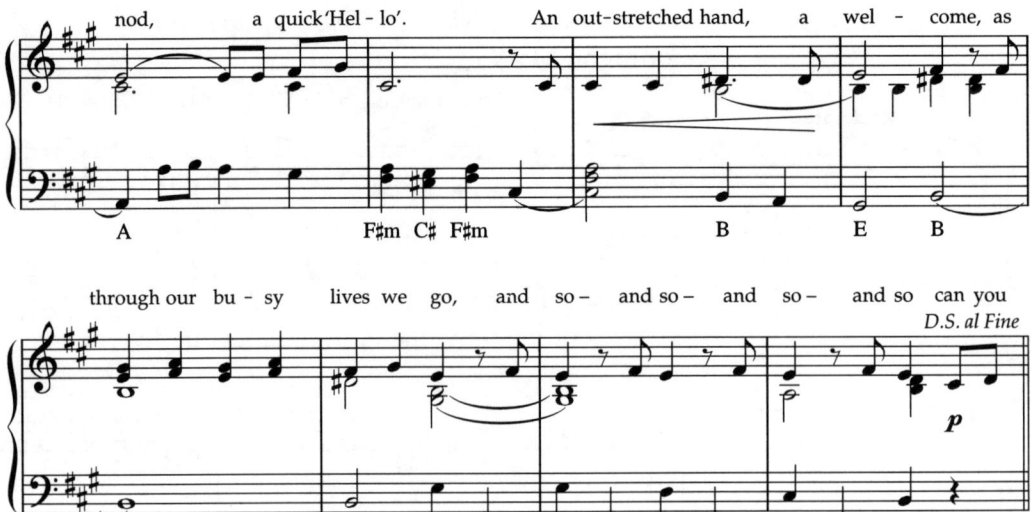

Can you spare a litle love,
a little smile, a little gladness?
Can you share a little friendliness,
help others on their way?
Lend a helping hand
and comfort one another.
Let in a ray of sunshine,
to brighten up the day.

For love is in the little things,
a nod, a quick 'Hello'.
An outstretched hand, a welcome,
as through our busy lives we go,
and so – and so – and so – and so

(Repeat verse 1 – Noel and children)

(Towards end of song, children begin to leave. Matthew is last to leave)

Noel Time for bed, Matthew. Thanks for letting me meet your friends. *(Picks up clipboard)* And tomorrow, you can help me finish my work.

Matthew Maybe I'll help you to find the Christmas spirit. *(Stifles a yawn)*

Noel *(Laughs and ruffles Matthew's hair)* I hope you do. Goodnight, Matthew.

Matthew Goodnight.

(Exit Matthew. Noel moves to corner of the stage. Lights out)

Narrator And so, the night before Christmas Eve, all the children went to bed and dreamed of Christmas. And when the street was quiet, only one light remained, only one person was awake . . .

(One light picks out the figure of Old Grumpy. He stands on steps, moves gradually to centre of stage)

Please call my name

*I hear the music – I hear the laughter
and with my mem'ries, I'm young again;
and in the distance, voices calling,
rememb'ring me – they call my name.*

1. A tattered coat, an empty shell.
   Once I was loved, and I was loved so well.
   A mother's arms around me twined,
   'beloved son of me and mine'
   – please call my name!

2. Make me someone, make me real,
   just glance at me – and then I'll feel
   I'm welcomed in – I'm one of you,
   just for a moment – a moment or two
   – please call my name!

Reprise for ending:
Won't you call my name?
Just call my name!

(A dim light picks out Noel watching Old Grumpy from the corner of the stage. At Reprise for ending he sings softly with him, Old Grumpy making his way back up the steps as he sings)

Please call my name

(Lights out – stage in darkness)

Narrator   Matthew was excited about Christmas and about his mysterious new friend, Noel. He wondered if they'd find the Spirit of Christmas – and if they did, what it would be like. At last, he fell asleep and dreamed about his friends singing carols, getting ready for Christmas.

(Dimmed light gradually illuminates stage. Chorus arranged in little huddles, sleeping. As introduction to song is played, they sit up, one by one, rubbing eyes, gradually awakening, they sing **Dreaming of Christmas***)*

DREAMING OF CHRISTMAS

1. We've been good, as good as can be,
   and we'll get our presents 'neath the Christmas tree,
   'cos we hear the bells on Santa's sleigh,
   and we know he's on his way.

   Dreaming, dreaming of Christmas,
   we'll be as good, as good as can be.
   Dreaming, dreaming of Christmas,
   and presents 'neath the Christmas tree.

2. Look at all the lovely toys,
   Santa's brought for girls and boys;
   a cuddly teddy, soft as can be,
   a soldier marching – one, two, three.

3. A pretty doll with golden curls,
   a spinning top that twists and twirls,
   Jack-in-the-Box who jumps with a pop,
   and a furry rabbit going hop, hop, hop.

DREAMING OF CHRISTMAS

DREAMING OF CHRISTMAS *continued* ...

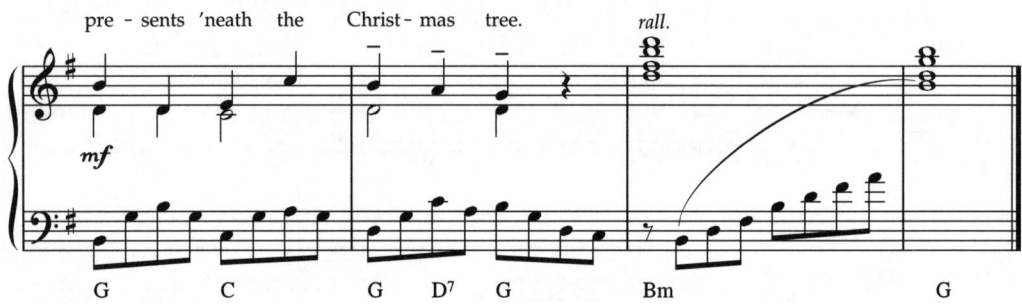

(Lights out – pause)
(Voices in the darkness. Key of G connects)

Voice 1   Ding dong, merrily on high,
in heav'n the bells are ringing ...

Voice 2   Good King Wenceslas looked out,
on the feast of Stephen ...

Voice 3   See amid the winter's snow,
born for us on earth below ...

Mitzi   *(tuneless)* Rudolph the red-nosed reindeer ...

Old Grumpy   *(Bellows, interrupting)* Be quiet! Pests, the lot of you!

Scene 2

(Lights go up – two children cross stage carrying long placard, emblazoned 'Christmas Eve'. Enter a group of children, talking excitedly, arguing among themselves)

Child 1   You *can't* be getting *all those things* for Christmas. Santa Claus wouldn't have room for our stuff if he had to carry *all of that*! It's just *not* fair; all those things for just one person!

Mitzi   *(Pushing to the front of the group)* I am getting *loads* of presents. And if Santa can't carry them all, my mum's buying extras at the shops.

Matthew   *(To child on fringe of group)* I'm getting a box of paints and books and maybe a football strip. What about you?

Child 2   *(Shakes head)* Dunno. Maybe I'll get . . .

Mitzi   *(Pushing forward again)* I'm getting *two* dolls, a pram, a doll's house, a new party dress – and . . .

Matthew   *(To child 2)* I'd really like roller blades, but they're a bit dangerous . . .

Mitzi   . . . and I'm getting a mountain bike . . .

(Group of children giggle. Enter Noel)

Noel   *(To Mitzi)* What else are you getting for Christmas?

(Mitzi takes a deep breath, looking pleased. Matthew tugs Noel's sleeve)

Matthew   Don't start her off again, Noel. She's always boasting.

Noel   What's your name?

Mitzi   *(Pleased at getting attention)* Mitzi – but my mummy and daddy call me their Little Princess!

(Groan from the other children. Then a door slams as Mrs Never-In bustles down the steps festooned in shopping bags. Pauses to give Mitzi a hug)

Mrs Never-In Just off to the shops, Princess. 'Won't be long. I need a few extra things!

Mitzi *(Holds on to her mum's coat)* Remember to bring *me* something, Mummy.

Mrs Never-In *(Fondly)* Of course, my poppet. Mummy never forgets her little Mitzi.

(Sound closely resembling 'yeuch' from Group)

Noel If you have too many Christmas presents, you won't enjoy them half as much as someone who has just one or two things.

Mitzi *(Shouts) Yes I will*!

Noel But you don't *need* all those things – dolls, a bicycle, a doll's house . . .

Mitzi *(Furious) Yes I do*! Well, maybe I don't, but . . .

I don't need it, but I want it and I'll get it!

I don't need it, but I want it and I'll get it!
And there won't be enough for two,
and if I'm disappointed, I'll bring them into line,
with a great big loud *boohoo*.

I don't need it, but I want it and I'll get it,
and I won't share any with you.
I can eat it or I'll wear it,
if I'm tired of it I'll tear it!

And if they stop my presents,
oh, I can promise you,
I'll throw a giant tantrum,
drum my heels upon the floor,
and make it a right *blue do*!

I don't need it, but I want it and I'll get it!

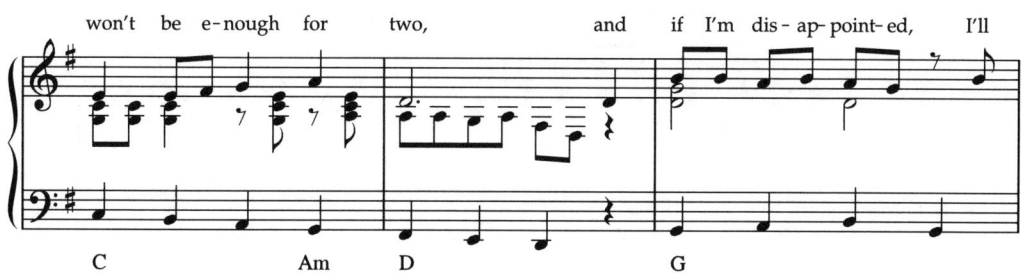

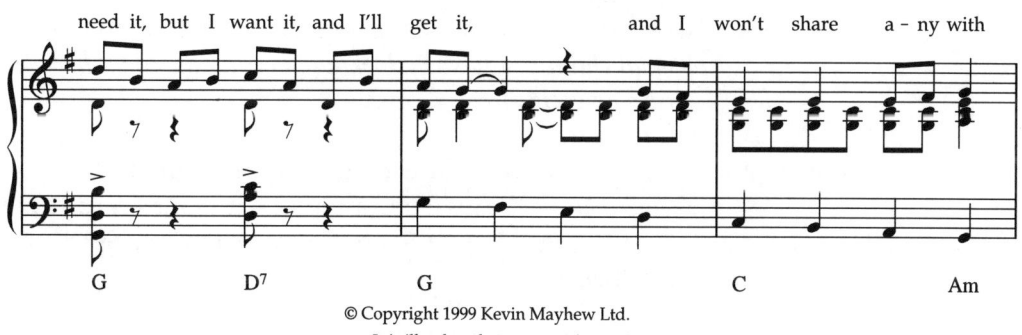

I DON'T NEED IT, BUT I WANT IT AND I'LL GET IT! *continued ...*

          (Mitzi leaves group, pops into her house and returns with large tin/jar of sweets. Sits on steps sampling them. A couple of small children approach, looking hopeful. She turns her back – keeps on eating)

Matthew   Come on, you two. Time to give out the Christmas cards. *(Aside to Noel)* We give one another Christmas cards now – 'cos we're getting quite grown up. Is that the Spirit of Christmas, Noel?

Noel   *(Laughs and sits down on steps, watching group pass a flurry of envelopes around)* Not quite, Matthew – but it's a good start.

Christmas card song

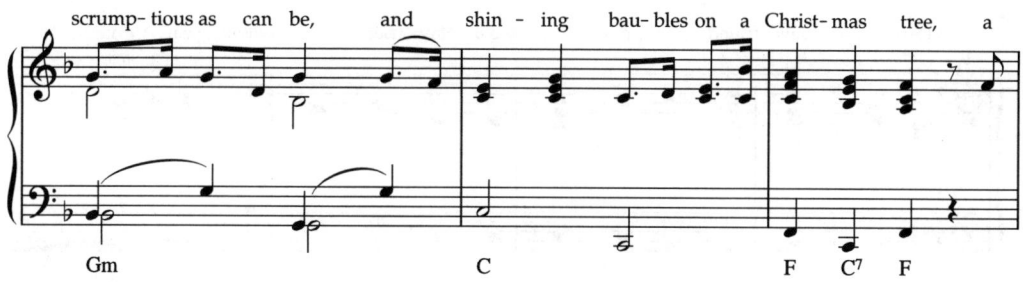
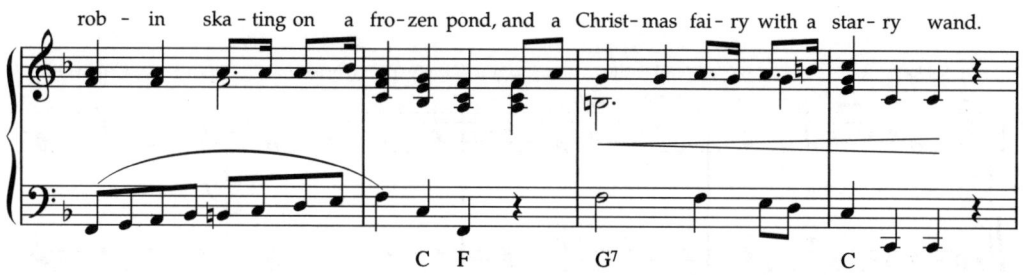

© Copyright 1999 Kevin Mayhew Ltd.
It is illegal to photocopy music.

CHRISTMAS CARD SONG *continued ...*

CHRISTMAS CARD SONG

1. Here's a Christmas pudding,
   scrumptious as can be,
   and shining baubles on a Christmas tree,
   a robin skating on a frozen pond,
   and a Christmas fairy with a starry wand.

2. Open the card and look inside,
   it's a jolly greeting for Christmastide.
   Peace and plenty, joy we send;
   This card is saying,
   'Let's be friends'.

3. Please be my friend for Christmas,
   we'll stay friends the whole year through.
   Don't forget to read the message:
   'Happy Christmas',
   'Happy Christmas',
   'Happy Christmas from me to you'.

(While children concentrate on cards, Mitzi puts down her tin/jar of sweets and appears to be crying, knuckles in eyes. Noel joins her)

Noel   What's the matter, Mitzi?

Mitzi   Nobody, *(sob)* gave *me* a Christmas card! *(sob)*

Noel   *(Shaking his head sadly)* And did you give a card to anyone else?

Mitzi   *(Indignantly)* No – why should I?

Noel   *(Pointing to tin)* And did you share your sweets?

Mitzi   *(Glaring, clutching sweets to her)* No – they're *mine*.

Noel   *(Gently)* Maybe it's because you were boasting about your Christmas presents.

Mitzi   *(Glaring at him)* I *like* presents.

Noel Do you need all those things, though? Maybe you could share them with somebody who has hardly any presents and that way, you could enjoy the *best* present of all.

Mitzi *(Looks puzzled) Best* present?

Noel Yes. The one that Baby Jesus gives to everyone at Christmas. Just think – it's *his* birthday – and he gives you a present.

Mitzi *(Attacking her sweets again)* What present?

Noel The gift of love, Mitzi. He gives it to us all. We have to remember that at Christmas. And d'you know what's so special about this particular present?

(Mitzi, munching, shakes her head)

Noel The more love you give to others, the more you have for yourself. Give it away, and *(he taps his chest)* it grows and grows inside you.

Mitzi What's that got to do with sharing my presents?

(Noel sighs, shakes his head)

(Matthew has been standing nearby, listening to the conversation. At one point, he disappears into his own house for approximately ten seconds, comes back, hands envelope to Mitzi)

Matthew Er – Happy Christmas, Mitzi. Er – I nearly forgot your card.

(Mitzi snatches card and glances at it)

Mitzi *It's horrible* – it's got a *kangaroo* on it. What's that got to do with Christmas?

Noel As much as . . . oh, never mind. Nice try, Matthew.

(Noel and Matthew walk together to centre stage)

Noel I thought you were going to help me today, Matthew.

Matthew Yes, I will. But why are you looking so sad, Noel?

Noel Well, my chances of finding the Spirit of Christmas seem to be growing less and less. And there's not much time left. It sort of – sort of –

Matthew Gets you down?

(Noel nods. Matthew suddenly tugs his hand)

Matthew Never mind. We'll cheer you up. We've been practising a special song – just for a change from Christmas carols. C'mon. We'll sing it to you – you can join in if you like. *Everybody* can join in. *(Smiles at audience)*

JESUS AND ME

Sing out! Sing the song of Jesus and me
Let me tell the world about Jesus and me.

He leads me and I follow,
he keeps me safe yet sets me free.
He gives me love, enough to share –
that's Jesus and me.

Ring out joyful bells,
gather round, O come and see,
that Love came down at Christmas,
for you and me.

Sing out! Sing the song of Jesus and me
Let me tell the world about Jesus and me.

He leads me and I follow,
he keeps me safe yet sets me free.
He gives me love, enough to share –
that's Jesus and me.

(At end of song, Noel is beaming)

JESUS AND ME

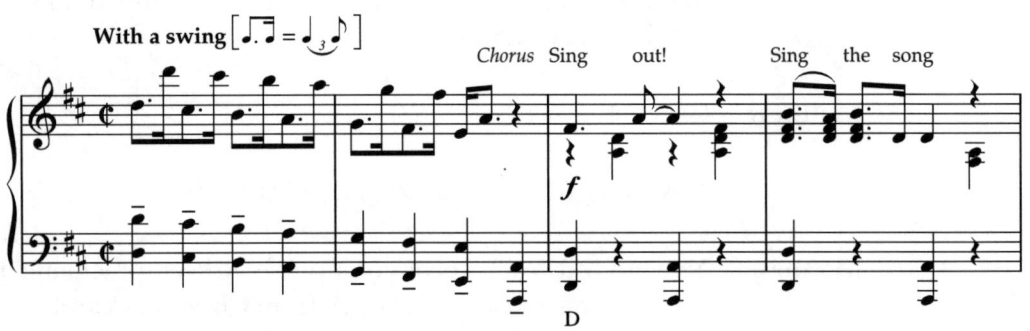
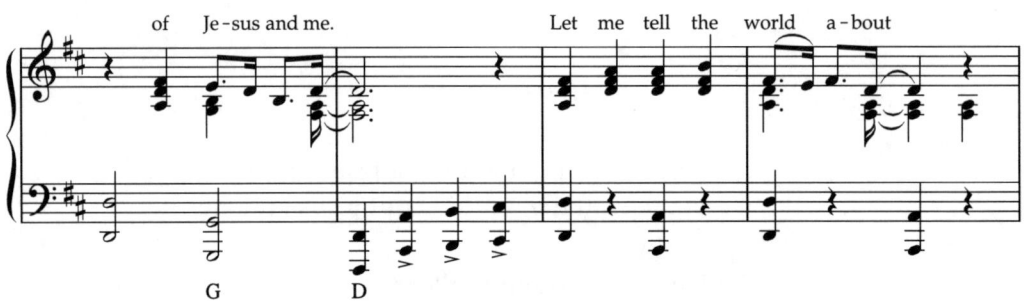
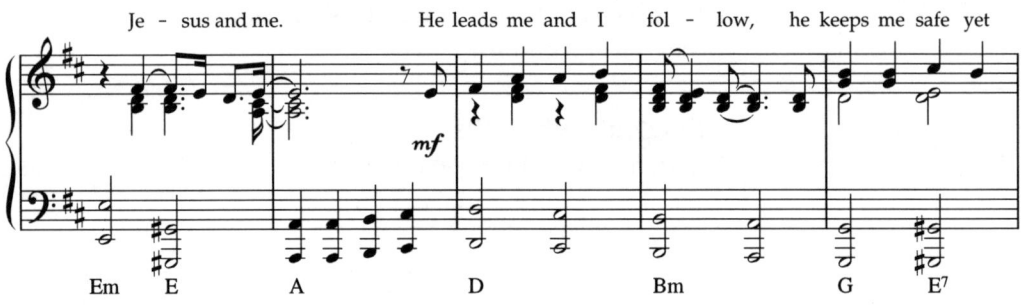

© Copyright 1999 Kevin Mayhew Ltd.
It is illegal to photocopy music.

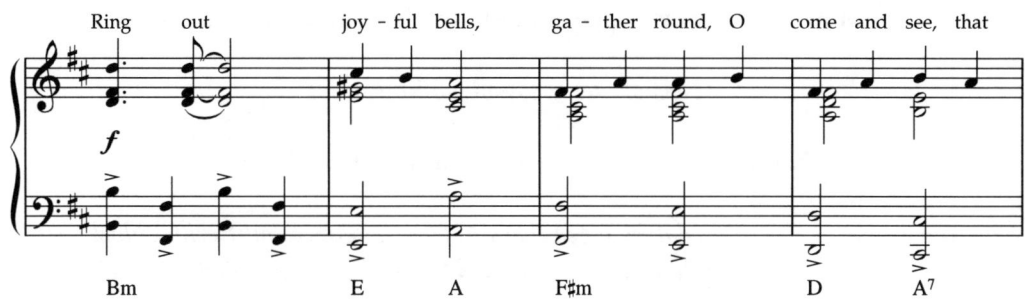

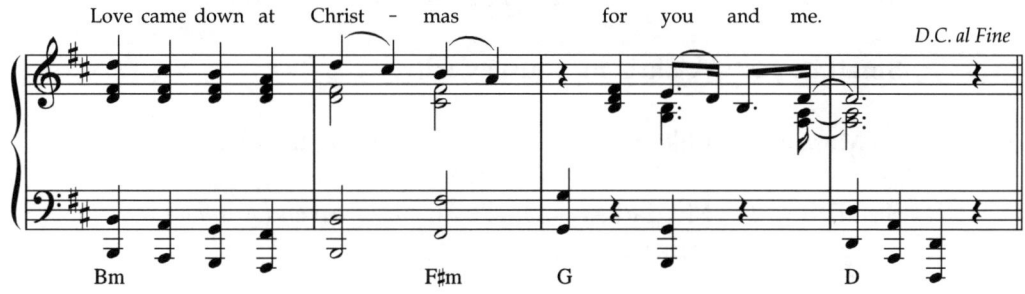

Noel   Thanks, everybody. I feel loads better. *You* all know about Christmas – your song told me that.

(Matthew and Noel go to centre stage. Children melt into the background – offstage or just unlit)

Matthew   *(Importantly)* Now, I'll show you round, so you can finish your Christmas survey.

(Noel lifts clipboard – leave it lying somewhere handy)

Matthew   I know *everybody* in this street.

Noel   Good. Give me their names.

Matthew   *(With large arm gestures, points to houses)*
One, Two, Three, Four, Five.
That's Five – Mrs High and Mighty.
That's Four, my house – Mum and Dad. My mum's called Eileen and my dad's called Jan.
That's Three, Mrs Next-Door – she's always busy.
And that's Two, Mrs Never-In – she's Mitzi's mum and she's always at the shops.
And that's One, *(hesitates)* em, Old Grumpy.

(Noel stares at him)

Matthew Sorry, I just don't know his name. Nobody does.

(Noel shakes his head, smiling)

Noel You wait here. I'll go and talk to them.

(Matthew goes back to friends. Lots of muttering. Noel goes to Old Grumpy's door. No reply. He leaves, shaking head)

Small Boy 1 That Noel's busy again. What's he doin'?

Small Boy 2 A Christmas survey, silly!

Matthew I like him. He's sort of – special, isn't he?

Small Boy 2 My dad says Noel's an *enig* – an *en* *(stumbles over the word)* an *enigma*.

(Chorus of 'What's that?')

(Mitzi's voice (raucous) floats in)

Mitzi I'm getting one of them for Christmas as well!

(Children groan. Watch Noel with interest)

Small Boy 2 Look. He's at Mrs High and Mighty's door. She'll *never* talk to him – she's having one of her swanky parties tonight.

(House lit. Noel knocks on door several times. Vision in glitter/boa, etc, comes out)

Narrator Mrs High and Mighty wasn't pleased to see Noel. She was getting ready for her sort of Christmas – a social whirl.

Noel *(Making notes)* And do you invite all your neighbours to your party?

Mrs High and Mighty What? Of course not! I invite *suitable* people.

Noel *(Politely)* And who are they – these *suitable* people?

Mrs High and Mighty Why, people like *us*, of course. Let me explain –

Elegance, etiquette

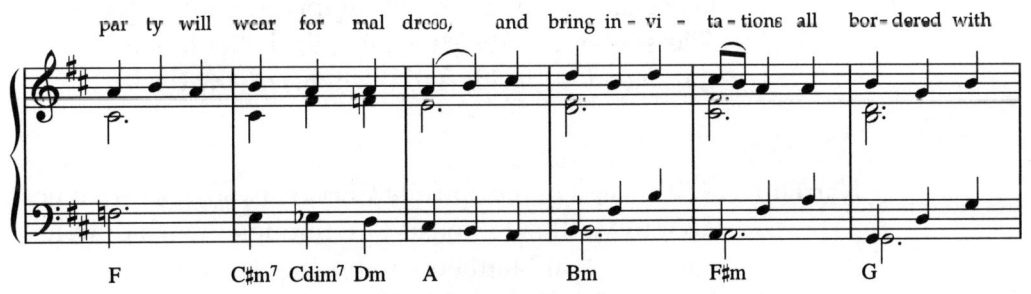

© Copyright 1999 Kevin Mayhew Ltd.
It is illegal to photocopy music.

ELEGANCE, ETIQUETTE continued ...

Elegance, etiquette, perfection for me:
I insist that I have matching lights on my tree;
With fine wines and canapés, I'm a social success.
The guests at my party will wear formal dress,
and bring invitations all bordered with gold.
Gatecrashers, my dear, will simply be told:
'Please stand on the pavement, the better to see
the splendour inside and the lights on my tree!'

Narrator Still no sign of the Spirit of Christmas, so Noel went next door to Matthew's house. But, through the window, he could see that Matthew's mum and dad were busy laying a Christmas table. He decided to go back later and went on to Mrs Next-Door.

(House lit. Knocks. Woman in overall, carrying baking bowl, comes to door, agitated)

Narrator Mrs Next-Door wasn't in a good mood. And she certainly didn't want to answer questions about Christmas.

Mrs Next-Door Christmas? Don't talk to me about Christmas. It's the same every year. Cooking for *days* before. The whole family comes for dinner on Christmas Day – running back and forward – skid marks on the kitchen floor – and *he (Jerks her head to where man in cap and slippers is reading a newspaper)* – *he* just sits there!

Noel *(Stepping back)* So, for you, Christmas means – means – *cooking*?

(Mrs Next-Door nods, hands baking bowl and whisk to Noel)

Mrs Next-Door Mphm! Cooking! I've got *twenty-one* coming for their dinner tomorrow! *(Nods at bowl)* Keep that goin' and I'll tell you about it!

(Noel meekly beats contents of bowl)

Twenty-one for Dinner

I've twenty-one for dinner,
I've far too much to do;
invited all the family
and Gran and Grandpa too.
I'm in a proper muddle,
in fact I have to say,
the one thing that I'd like to do
is miss out Christmas Day!

'Cos, with turkey and with Christmas cake,
I'm cooking endlessly,
and *he* won't even clear the plates,
but snores beneath the tree.
Tomorrow? That's a nightmare,
and Christmas just a blur.
I feel like running miles away,
that would create a stir . . . 'cos
I've twenty-one for dinner!

Twenty-one for Dinner

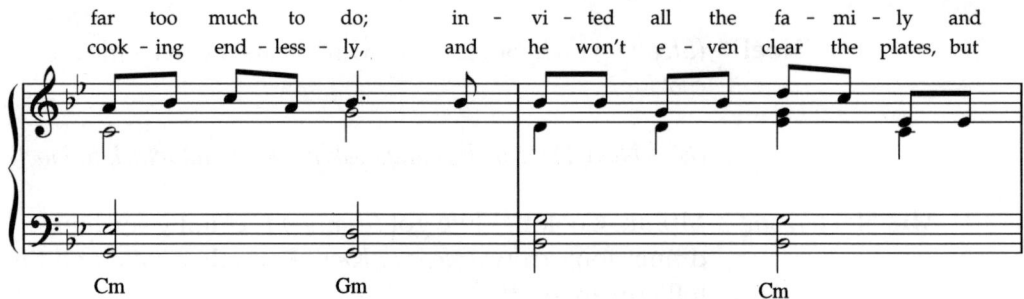

© Copyright 1999 Kevin Mayhew Ltd.
It is illegal to photocopy music.

(Noel hands back bowl as song ends. Mrs Next-Door goes indoors. Noel goes towards Mrs Never-In's house)

Narrator Noel went on to Mrs Never-In's door – but she wasn't in! He met her just as he came down the garden path. She'd been to the shops – again.

(Noel meets Mrs Never-In, laden with shopping, breathless. Speaks to her)

Mrs Never-In Christmas for me is shopping. Love it. Wouldn't miss it for anything. The shops are full of *lovely* things, aren't they? Here – hold these parcels, and I'll tell you about it.

(Thrusts parcels at Noel)

LAST-MINUTE SHOPPING

Last-minute shopping,
rushing round the stores,
no matter what I've gone and bought,
I always need to buy some more.
My purse is nearly empty,
my cheque book's nearly done:
my credit cards are melting;
But I'm having so much fun,
that I will shop! shop! shop until I drop,
and I'll have a merry Christmas.

Shop! shop! shop until I drop,
and I'll have a merry Christmas!

Last-Minute Shopping

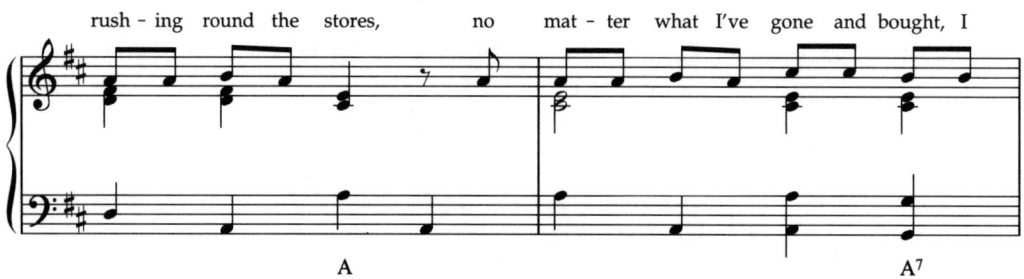

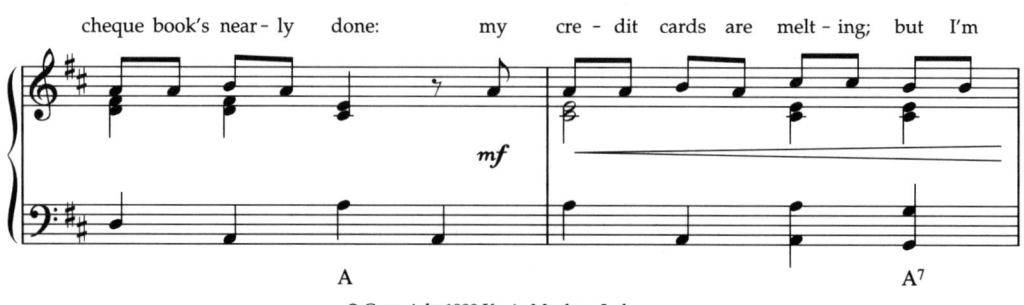

© Copyright 1999 Kevin Mayhew Ltd.
It is illegal to photocopy music.

(*She finishes her song with a flourish and disappears into her house. Noel sits on steps, writing on his clipboard, looking rather dejected. Matthew joins him, peering over his shoulder at the clipboard*)

Matthew Any luck? Have you found the Spirit of Christmas?

Noel No. Cooking, shopping, posh parties, people expecting lots of presents – but not the real Spirit of Christmas. (*He sighs*)

Matthew What is the Spirit of Christmas, Noel?

Noel It has to do with love, Matthew. You see, love came down at Christmas. Jesus is love, and where there is love – well – how can I explain it? (*Thinks for a moment*) It lights up our world, just like the Christmas star that shone as baby Jesus was born.

SHINE, CHRISTMAS STAR

(*Noel sings*)

Remember love,
so we can journey safely onward;
keep it safe and think of Christmas night.
When winter winds blew cold and chill,
in silence here the earth stood still.
Then love was born, the star shone out
and bathed our world in light.

Matthew And if we find love?

(*Noel smiles and sings*)

A star still shines
to lead us to a bright tomorrow,
beaming out so we can find a way
to make a world where kindness lives,
a world where we can give
the gift of love to others,
a place where love will stay.

Shine, Christmas Star
shine, Christmas Star
and make a world,
a world where love forever stays.

(*Both repeat second verse and refrain. Sit for a moment in silence*)

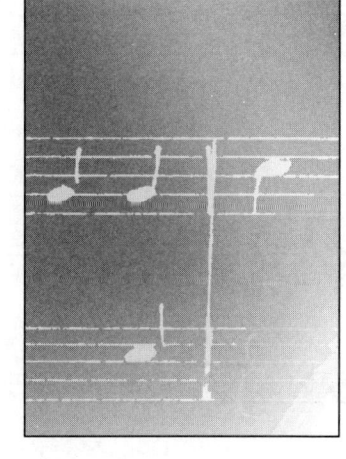

SHINE CHRISTMAS STAR

Matthew *(Eagerly)* Maybe you'll find the Spirit of Christmas at our house. You haven't been there yet, have you?

Noel Your mum and dad were busy. I'll go back in a little while. My *last* visit, Matthew.

(Matthew sits down beside him)

Matthew At Christmas, in our house, we have *customs*.

(Noel looks enquiring)

Matthew *Old customs*. Like – my mum lights a big candle on Christmas Eve and puts it in the highest window of the house, and it burns there 'till Christmas morning. It's to welcome Baby Jesus. *(Gestures here)*

Noel *(Interested)* That's a lovely custom, Matthew.

Matthew *(Pleased, nods)* That's 'cos my grandad was from Ireland. It's an Irish custom – and my other grandad was Polish. So that's why we have our big Christmas meal on Christmas *Eve* instead of Christmas Day – and we set an extra place at the table.

Noel An extra place?

Matthew *(Eagerly)* Yes . . . and that's for 'the stranger' . . . well . . . anyone who has no place to go at Christmas . . . or anyone who knocks on the door and asks for help on Christmas Eve . . . or anyone who's lost or lonely at Christmas . . . or anyone . . .

(Noel smiles, puts up a restraining hand)

Noel Right, Matthew. I get the general idea. What a lovely custom.

(Matthew looks pleased. Eileen appears at door of house, holding a lit candle, calls to Matthew)

Eileen Come, Matthew. It's time to put the candle in the window to welcome Baby Jesus . . .

(Sees Noel and moves down to centre stage)

Eileen Noel . . . you can come too. Now that our Christmas table is ready it's time to . . .

(Holds out the candle)

Noel Yes . . . Matthew has told me all about your customs. I did so enjoy hearing about them. But *(points to candle)* tell me about this just once more.

(Eileen smiles. Holds candle aloft and sings)

A LIGHT AT MY WINDOW

A light at my window, to welcome the Christ child,
to show weary travellers the path to my door.
A guide in the dark for the lost and the lonely,
in his name a welcome: 'God save you, asthore'.*

The light is my prayer and my hope is his blessing.
O grant that his peace may be given to me.
May our home be a shelter from storms
that surround us.
May the love that he brings in our hearts ever be,
may the love that he brings in our hearts ever be.

* Irish/Gaelic: 'my dear'

(Holds candle as she sings. Turns as song ends. Goes to put candle in window. Matthew follows her, but stops outside the house. Looks back at Noel. Beckons. Noel joins Matthew. Goes into house with Jan. Enter Old Grumpy stage left)

A LIGHT AT MY WINDOW

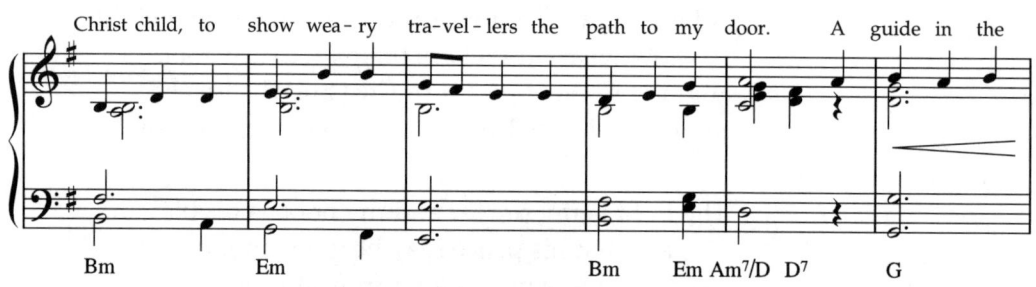
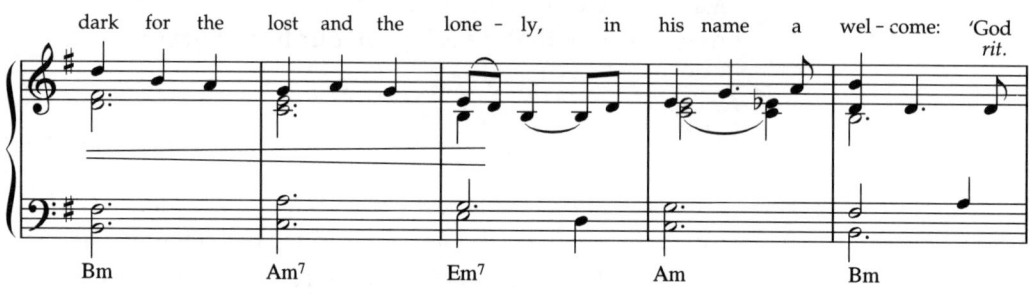

*Irish/Gaelic: 'my dear'.

© Copyright 1999 Kevin Mayhew Ltd.
It is illegal to photocopy music.

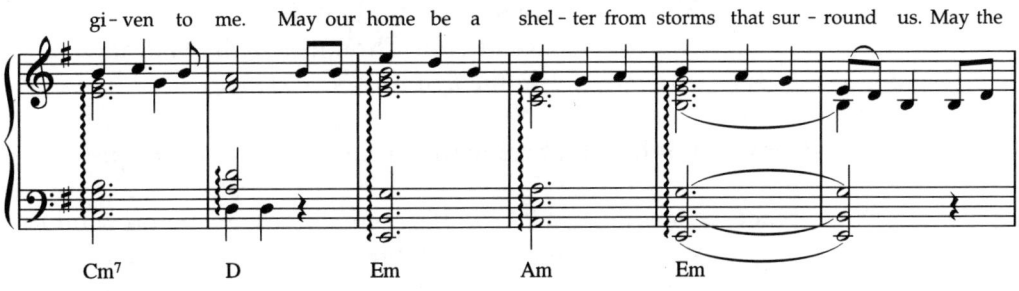
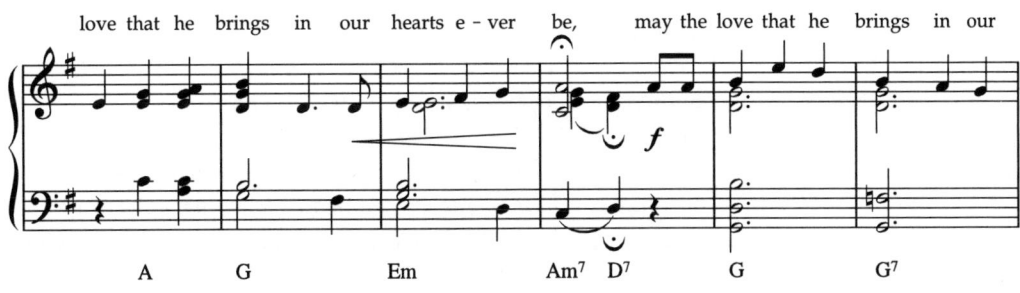

Narrator	And in the shadows, someone was watching. Someone who had been forgotten in all the excitement on Christmas Eve. And as Matthew's father showed Noel the Christmas table and explained the custom of the extra place laid there, the old man who watched sang a snatch of his song again, feeling sure that no one would hear him – or even notice him.
	(Old Grumpy sings 'A tattered coat, etc'. Lights dim – front stage. Matthew and Noel return to centre stage)
Noel	Now I'm happy. I've found the true Spirit of Christmas. My work is finished – and I know just the person to fill that extra place at your Christmas table, Matthew. *(Points to retreating figure of Old Grumpy)*
Matthew	But he won't come to our house – he *hates* people.
Noel	He will – if you call his name, Matthew. If you want to welcome him to your table, I'll tell you his name. *(Matthew nods eagerly. Noel bends to whisper in his ear)*
	(Background music – softly repeats **Please call my name***)*
	(Matthew runs towards Old Grumpy as he goes back to his house)
Matthew	*Benjamin, Benjamin.* Wait, wait, *Benjamin*!
	(Old Grumpy turns, slowly smiles, takes Matthew's outstretched hand – rather slow motion, mime effect, and allows himself to be led to Matthew's door, where Eileen and Jan welcome him.)
Matthew	Here's my new friend – he's called Benjamin.
Jan	Come in, come in and be our honoured guest. Come – see the good things we have to eat. Welcome to our home, Benjamin – and a Happy Christmas.
	(Noel smiles, nods approvingly, then walks to side of stage making notes)
	(Eileen, Jan and Matthew usher Benjamin to his place at table. Enter Mrs Next-Door, in apron and slippers, smeared in flour. She is carrying a large jug. Speaks to Noel)

Mrs Next-Door	What'll I do, what'll I do? I'm stuck! All the shops are shut and I've run out of milk.
Noel	Don't worry. I'm sure Eileen will give you some. Go on . . . ask her.
Mrs Next-Door	But I hardly know her . . . it looks as if she's busy . . . and she's got company.

(Noel takes her arm; propels her towards Eileen's door)

Noel	This is a perfect way to get to know your neighbour. She's really nice *(gives her a slight push)* . . . go on. *(Mrs Next-Door meets Eileen in the doorway. They talk. Eileen smiles and takes the jug)*
Eileen	Twenty-one for dinner . . . and they're all your own family . . . sons, daughters, cousins, uncles, aunts . . . ? *No* outsiders allowed? Well . . . I suppose with a great big family like that . . . all those relations . . . it'll be difficult to include anyone else at Christmas. And all that preparation? Why . . . you must be exhausted.

(Mrs Next-Door nods wearily)

Mrs Next-Door	'Fraid so. And I must say, what with all this cooking and baking . . . it doesn't feel like Christmas.

(Eileen takes her arm)

Eileen	Come on . . . take a little break from it all. Come in and help us enjoy our Christmas Eve celebration. Don't be a Catering Victim.

(Noel approaches)

Noel	She's right. You've made enough food to feed a regiment. All you have to do now is prepare a warm welcome . . . and you can do that tomorrow.

(Mrs Next-Door whips off her apron, pats her hair and goes in with Eileen. Sounds of celebration from Eileen's house. Noel continues to make notes. Enter Mrs Never-In . . . half running . . . laden with parcels. Suddenly stumbles. Sinks down in a heap with parcels. Matthew is peeping out of the window. He rushes out. He and Noel help Mrs Never-In to her feet)

Mrs Never-In	Oh dear. I just came over all faint there. Too much rushing about I expect.
Matthew	I'll go and get you a glass of water.
Mrs Never-In	Thank you, Matthew. You're a good boy.
Noel	*(taking her arm)* Come and sit down. Have a bit of a rest.

(Noel looks at her pile of parcels)

Noel	Tell me . . . was it worth it? All this rushing about and Christmas shopping, I mean.

(Matthew brings glass of water. Mrs Never-In sips it)

Mrs Never-In	To answer your question . . .

*(Song intro here. Same tune as **Last-Minute Shopping** but sung much more slowly)*

SHOP UNTIL I DROP

Last-minute shopping, rushing round the stores,
no matter what I've gone and bought
I always need to buy some more.
My purse is nearly empty,
my cheque book's nearly done,
my credit cards are melting,
but I'm having so much 'fun',
that I will shop, shop, shop until I drop,
and I'll have a merry Christmas!

The crush of the shoppers,
the ringing of the tills,
my credit card's on overload,
I'm dreading January's bill.
Got caught up in a frenzy,
I'm in . . . and I want out.
Buying everything in sight,
can't be what Christmas is about.

I've shopped, shopped, shopped until I dropped
and I'll have an awful Christmas!

(Mrs Never-In ends her song, puts head in hands)

SHOP UNTIL I DROP

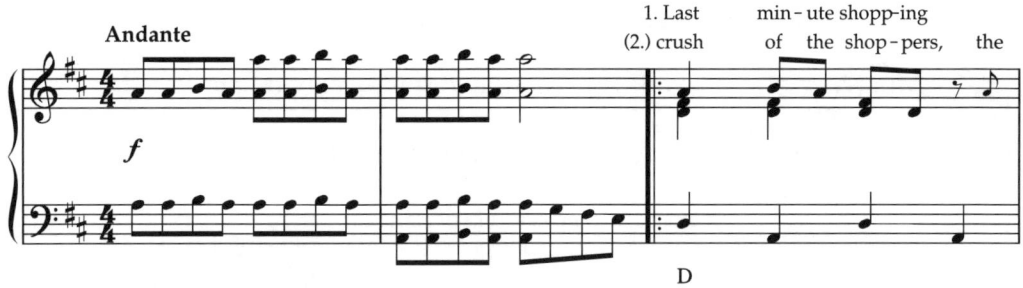
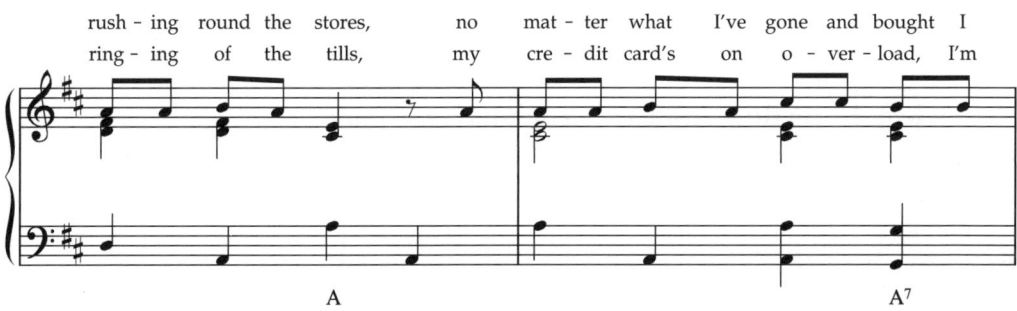

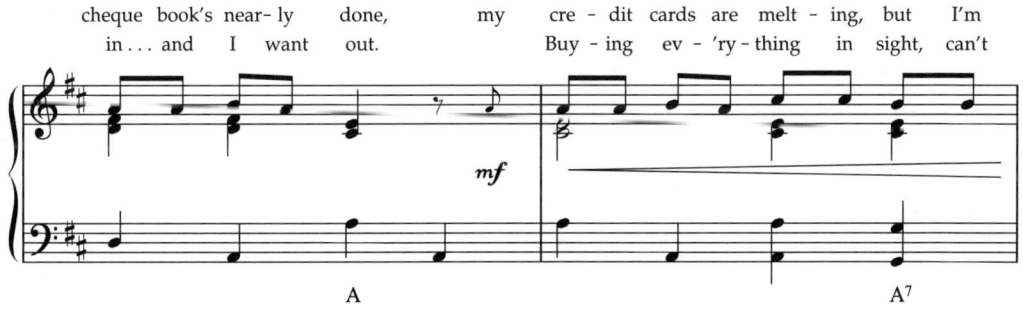

© Copyright 1999 Kevin Mayhew Ltd.
It is illegal to photocopy music.

Shop until I drop *continued . . .*

Matthew	Don't cry . . . please don't cry. It's Christmas! Look . . . I'll carry all your parcels home for you, and . . .

(Eileen comes from house. Mrs Never-In gets up, hands her the empty glass)

Eileen	Feeling better? Would you like to come up to the house for a while? Some of the neighbours have come in and we're all getting into the spirit of Christmas. I expect there'll be some carols later.

(Mrs Never-In begins to demur. Eileen persists. Noel nods encouragingly)

Eileen	Please come and join us. Jan and I . . . and Matthew haven't lived here very long, and this is giving us a chance to get to know our neighbours . . . including you. Come on . . . you're most welcome.

(Matthew gathers up the parcels)

Matthew	They're getting into the spirit of Christmas because Noel says that the Spirit of Christmas lives in our house, y'know.

(The others smile)

Mrs Never-In	Thank you. You've all been so kind. I'll come for a little while.
Matthew	And when I take the parcels to your house, I'll ask Mr Never- . . . er, your husband . . . er, Mitzi's dad if she can come along too.

(Exit Matthew. Eileen and Mrs Never-In go towards house where there are sounds of celebration. At the last minute, Eileen looks over her shoulder)

Eileen	Noel . . . you must be cold out here. Why don't you come as well?
Noel	*(Laughs)* Thank you . . . but I can't. I've completed my work, so I'll have to move on tonight. 'Back to base' I think they call it. And in the meantime . . . *(Laughs again)* . . . it looks as if I'm needed out here to direct the traffic . . . to your house.

(*Upstage, Mrs High and Mighty's door opens. She appears, still dressed in her party clothes but looking irritated. She addresses Noel, pointing to Eileen's house. As she speaks, she moves forward to join Noel*)

Mrs High and Mighty What's going on over there? Are they having a party? (*Strains of Christmas carols drift from the house*) (*Snorts*) Carols are for singing in church anyway. It doesn't seem a very sophisticated party to me. And can't they afford a tree? Just look at *that* . . . one little candle burning in the top window . . . really!

Noel The carols and the candle . . . all of them are a welcome for the Christ child. And I was just thinking . . . wouldn't it be wonderful if *everybody*, the world over, made that sort of gesture at Christmas? Forgot all the trimmings that have nothing to do with the birth of the Saviour . . . and got it right, just for once?

(*Mrs High and Mighty looks discomfited*)

Mrs High and Mighty Maybe you're right. Perhaps it's time for a change of direction . . . for me, at least. All that work for a party . . . no appreciation from the guests . . . I wish I hadn't bothered!

Noel And, by the way . . . if you're the hostess at your party . . . shouldn't you be looking after your guests?

Mrs High and Mighty They've gone. Off to another party. Hardly a word of thanks . . . just boasting about all the *social events* they'll be attending over Christmas. They're very full of themselves, you know.

(*Noel stifles a smile*)

Noel That's what you call self-congratulation, I believe. Not a pretty sight, they tell me.

(*Mrs High and Mighty gives a flourish of her feather boa and breaks into song – tune –* **Elegance, Etiquette**)

A BIG ANTI-CLIMAX

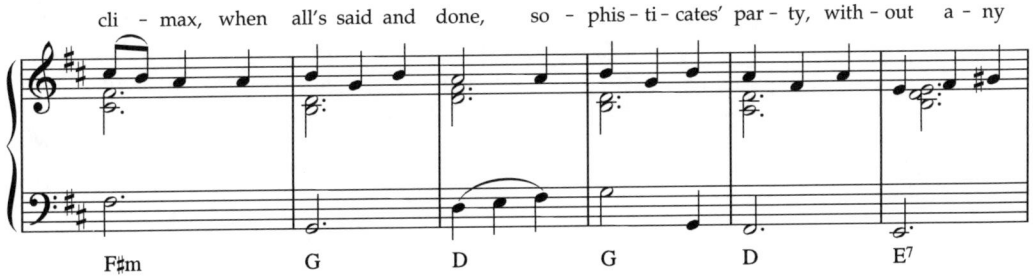

© Copyright 1999 Kevin Mayhew Ltd.
It is illegal to photocopy music.

A BIG ANTI-CLIMAX continued...

A big anti-climax,
when all's said and done,
sophisticates' party, without any fun.
The guests bored and boring,
quite snobbish . . . to me.
Despite all my efforts, it's easy to see,
that I've been so misguided, quite foolish as well.
There's something I've missed,
I'm quite sure . . . I can tell.
I know deep inside that there really must be,
much more to a Christmas, than lights on a tree!

(Song ends. She turns away, boa drooping, looking dejected, then hesitates, glancing up at Eileen's house. Gusts of laughter are coming through the open door. Sighs . . .)

Noel I suppose you've lots of food left over from your party.

Mrs High and Mighty Trays and trays of savouries . . . I can tell you . . . if I *never* slice a mushroom again it'll be too soon!

(Noel smiles)

Noel I've had an idea. I think that your neighbour Eileen would appreciate some of that left-over food. She's had lots of unexpected guests this evening you know. . .

(Mrs High and Mighty hesitates, looks at the house again, then thoughtfully at Noel)

Mrs High and Mighty I suppose you're right. A touch of the Christmas spirit wouldn't go amiss. I'll go and get the savouries.

(Goes back to her house. Returns to Eileen's door. Speaks to her. Invited in. Bearing her gift of party food, disappears into house)

(Voices off)

Mitzi What's *happened*? Where's my mum?

Matthew I've told you all about that, Mitzi. She's at our house. We're having a sort of party . . . you're invited too.

Mitzi Don't want to go. I'm waiting for my presents.

Matthew Come *on*, Mitzi. Come *on* . . . *(Enter Matthew and Mitzi. Mitzi tugs Noel's sleeve as Matthew runs eagerly to his house)*

Mitzi What's going on, Noel . . . up there? *(Points to Matthew's house)*

Noel Just some people celebrating Christmas by sharing what they have . . . by being kind to one another.

(Mitzi looks doubtful. Matthew turns at the open door and waves. Noel gives Mitzi a gentle push)

Noel Go on, Mitzi. Try some sharing . . . you'll enjoy it.

Mitzi *(Doubtfully)* Promise?

Noel I promise. Now . . . off you go.

(Mitzi joins Matthew)

Narrator And so the neighbours prepared for Christmas. Benjamin had a wonderful time and they all discovered that he loved singing. In fact, he taught them a little Christmas carol from long ago. *(Jan, Eileen, Matthew and their guests come out and stand centre stage, making their farewells)* Benjamin . . . sing us that little Christmas carol again.

SING GLORIA

Listen to the angel voices,
skies flood now with glorious light.
Heav'n resounds and earth rejoices,
Christ is born this Christmas night.
Gloria, sing gloria.
Peace on earth, goodwill to men.
Gloria, sing Gloria.
Christ is born in Bethlehem.

(Benjamin sings, others repeat. They shake hands and embrace taking their leave)

Sing gloria

© Copyright 1999 Kevin Mayhew Ltd.
It is illegal to photocopy music.

All	Thank you, Eileen, Jan. Thank you, Matthew.
Mrs Never-In	You've given us so much tonight . . . and I feel awful because I came to visit empty-handed.

(Eileen shakes her head)

Eileen	But we didn't plan it. And we shared the Spirit of Christmas . . . you all brought that to the party . . . and that's the best gift of all.
Mitzi	Wait, wait! I've had an idea . . . be back in a minute. *(Rushes off)*

(Mrs Next-Door takes Benjamin's hand)

Mrs Next-Door	I've had an idea as well.

(Sings. Same tune as previous song for Mrs Next-Door)

I've twenty-one for dinner,
but I know just what to do,
I'd like to make it twenty-two,
. . . so I'm inviting you!

(Speaks) Come for your Christmas dinner, Benjamin.

(Benjamin bows in a courtly fashion)

Benjamin	Thank you, dear lady. Who could resist an invitation in song?

(All laugh. As they leave, enter Mitzi with a large box. Gives it to Eileen)

Mitzi	A present for you. Thank you for the party. I just wanted to share some of my sweets with you, you see.

(Eileen smiles)

Eileen	Thank you so much, Mitzi. What a thoughtful little girl you are.

(Mitzi leaves, smiling broadly at the audience. Noel writes something on his clipboard with a flourish, and beams)

Noel That's it . . . complete.

(Noel slips away as guests leave. Jan is visible, clearing up in the house. Eileen and Matthew stand centre stage, Eileen with her arm around Matthew's shoulders)

Matthew *(Looking around)* He's gone, Mum. Noel's gone . . . *(Rushes from side to side of stage, looking for his friend)*

Eileen *(Quietly)* Matthew . . . come here. I want to explain something to you.

Narrator And so Noel had disappeared just as suddenly as he had come. Matthew was upset and puzzled, but his Mother was wise and seemed to understand. She comforted her son.

Eileen Don't cry, Matthew. Noel came, I think, as a sort of messenger. Now that his work is done, you won't see him again – but he'll be there – watching – especially at Christmas.

(Children and other cast members come in quietly and sit at side of stage)

Matthew Mum, do you think that Noel was an . . . an angel?

Eileen Who knows, Matthew? But maybe he was . . .

(Matthew smiles up at her)

Eileen It's past your bedtime, Matthew.

(Turns to the children, smiling)

Eileen . . . and you should have been asleep long ago!

(Murmur of dissent from the children)

Eileen But before you go to bed, I'll sing you a little Christmas song called **Close your Eyes**. Gather round, children . . .

CLOSE YOUR EYES

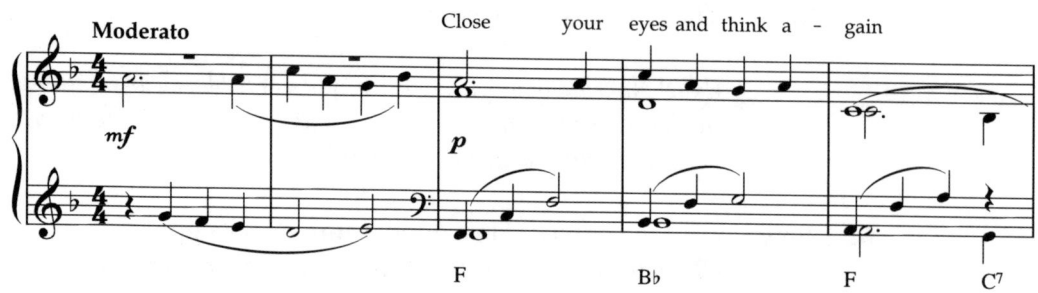
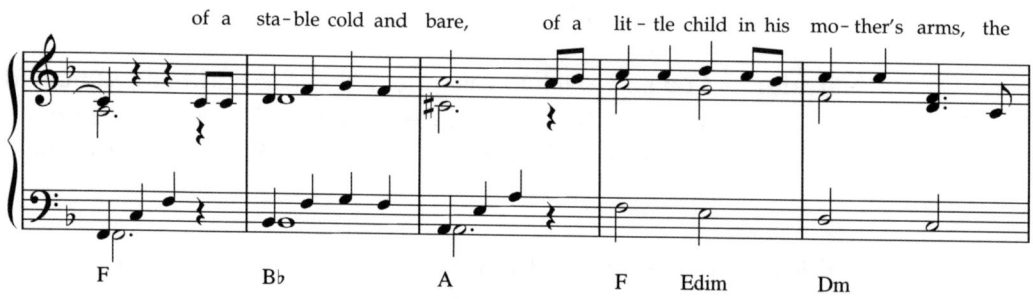
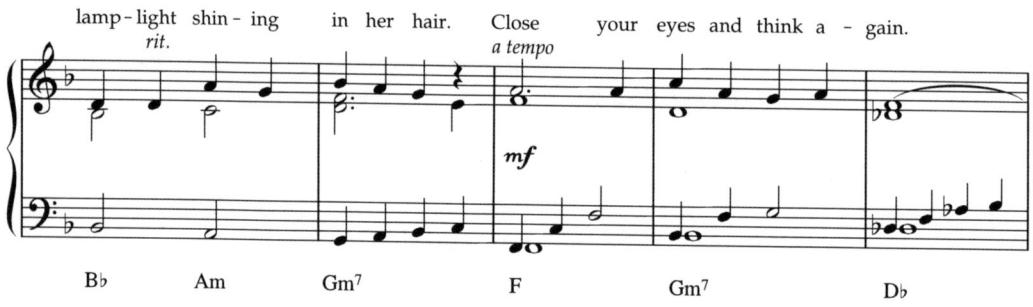

© Copyright 1999 Kevin Mayhew Ltd.
It is illegal to photocopy music.

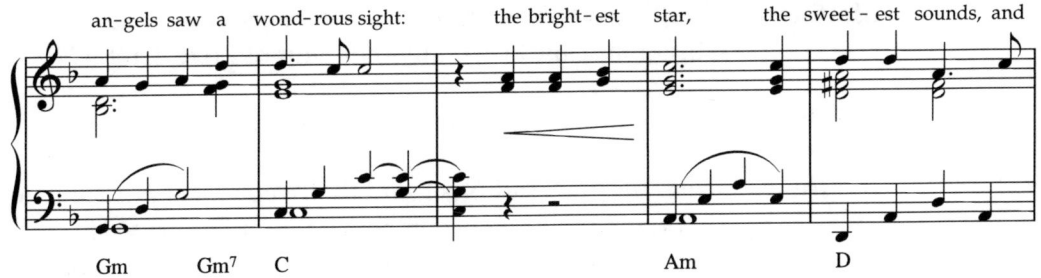

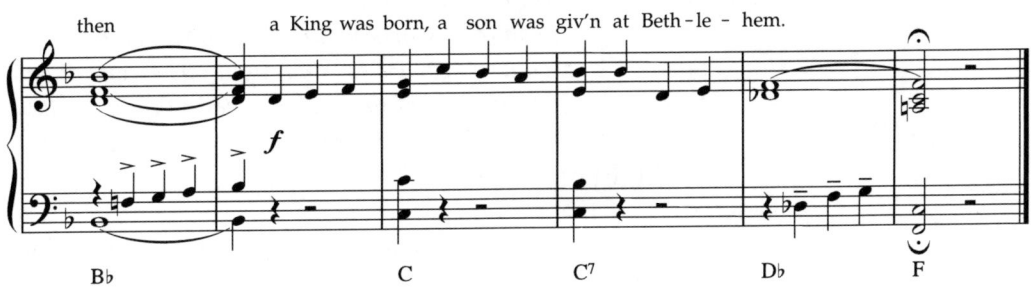

Close your eyes and think again
of a stable cold and bare,
of a little child in his mother's arms,
the lamplight shining in her hair.
Close your eyes and think again.

Close your eyes, remember Christmas night,
when earth stood still
and angels saw a wondrous sight:
the brightest star, the sweetest sounds,
and then a King was born, a son was giv'n at Bethlehem.

*(All form a little group centre stage. Children cover their eyes with their hands as Eileen sings **Close your Eyes**. Eileen sings song once through. Children repeat it with eyes open. As they sing, Eileen covers her eyes).*

Narrator And remembering all that Noel had said about God's Christmas gift of love, Matthew did one last thing for his friend, something which he knew would please him.

Matthew *(Points to candle in highest window of his house)* The Christmas candle is really the Light of Love, isn't it?

Eileen Yes, Matthew . . . it's what we call a *symbol*.

Matthew *(Nods eagerly)* And Noel said that we must share the love that the Baby Jesus brings to us, didn't he? *(Turns to friends. Murmur of agreement)* Well, we *will* share it. And we'll call it the Light of Love.

(Eileen brings the candle from the house. Children bring candles, light them from Christmas Candle, go down to audience – six children each side – and light one candle at end of each row. Each member of the audience has a taper/candle and the light is passed along the rows while cast on stage sing **The Light of Love***)*

(Noel sings solo verses offstage. Children gesture towards him, holding candles aloft, as he sings)

THE LIGHT OF LOVE

Chorus We offer you the Light of Love,
we offer you the Light of Love,
Take it and share it,
guard it and proudly bear it.
We offer you the Light of Love.

Noel Love is patient, love is kind.
Love, the gift of the Lord.
Now may we share it,
one with another,
and listen to his word.

Chorus We offer you the Light of Love,
we offer you the Light of Love . . .

Noel Listen to that small, still voice:
'I will be with you for all time,
close I will hold you,
deep I will love you,
remember . . . you are mine.'

We offer you the Light of Love,
we offer you the Light of Love . . .

THE LIGHT OF LOVE

THE LIGHT OF LOVE *continued ...*

Narrator   And so, in an ordinary street on Christmas Eve, an angel found the Spirit of Christmas. Happy Christmas to you all! *(Holds candle aloft)* And let the Light of Love shine the whole year through.

(The cast hold their candles aloft and sing)

Christmas blessing

© Copyright 1999 Kevin Mayhew Ltd.
It is illegal to photocopy music.

CHRISTMAS BLESSING

Joy be with you, peace enfold you,
love come down this Christmas night,
may your hearts be full of gladness.
May the Christ child bring you blessings,
may you walk within his light.

Joy be with you, peace enfold you,
love come down this Christmas night,
may your hearts be full of gladness.
May the Christ child bring you blessings,
may you walk within his light.

THE END